SMARTER WITH RUBIK'S CUBE

EVERYTHING YOUR KIDS NEED TO KNOW TO SOLVE
THE RUBIK'S CUBE

HARRINGTON YEH

Copyright 2021 - All rights reserved.

The content contained within this book may not be reproduced, duplicated or transmitted without direct written permission from the author or the publisher. Under no circumstances will any blame or legal responsibility be held against the publisher, or author, for any damages, reparation, or monetary loss due to the information contained within this book, either directly or indirectly.

Legal Notice:

This book is copyright protected. It is only for personal use. You cannot amend, distribute, sell, use, quote or paraphrase any part, or the content within this book, without the consent of the author or publisher.

Disclaimer Notice:

Please note the information contained within this document is for educational and entertainment purposes only. All effort has been executed to present accurate, up to date, reliable, complete information. No warranties of any kind are declared or implied. Readers acknowledge that the author is not engaged in the rendering of legal, financial, medical or professional advice. The content within this book has been derived from various sources. Please consult a licensed professional before attempting any techniques outlined in this book.

By reading this document, the reader agrees that under no circumstances is the author responsible for any losses, direct or indirect, that are incurred as a result of the use of the information contained within this document, including, but not limited to, errors, omissions, or inaccuracies.

CONTENTS

Introduction   5

1. For Parents – Why Every Kid Needs to Learn   11
   How to Solve the Rubik's Cube
2. History of the Rubik's Cube   20
3. Fun Facts About the Rubik's Cube   36
4. Why Should You Be Solving the Rubik's Cube?   51
5. All About Rubik's Cube Notations   59
6. How to Make a Flower Pattern with the Rubik's   66
   Cube
7. Making the White Cross   74
8. Solving the Bottom Corners of the First Layer   81
9. Solving Second Layer Edges   92
10. Solving the Last Layer Edges   99
11. Solving the Last Layer Corners   113
12. Some Tips on How to Solve the Rubik's Cube   121
    More Quickly
13. A Quick Recap of All the Algorithms   132

Conclusion   137

INTRODUCTION

So, you are having a "Show Your Talent" competition at school, where you hope to shine bright with your awesome dance moves and even secretly hope to win the first prize!

While hula-hooping is excellent, and so is being able to juggle three balls at a time, it is going to be impossible to compete with the charm of a 10-year-old who can perform Michael Jackson's moonwalk like a pro (alright, not really!).

The D-day comes, and you are ready to put your best foot forward, like literally. You have already seen the performances before you, and yes, all of them were wonderful. But you know that your chances of getting the top slot are high.

The curtains rise with colossal applause and fall with an even more deafening one once your performance is over.

You are smiling from ear to ear until you notice your classmate getting on stage with just a RUBIK'S CUBE in hand—and you're intrigued.

The following few seconds you just watch in amazement as she manages to solve that thing that you've struggled with for hours. *She solves it in a little less than 1 minute!* You can't help feeling a bit awe-struck (a little jealous even) as you join the rest of the crowd in applauding her genius.

Oh, and no prizes for guessing who won the competition!

Long story short: Kids who can solve the Rubik's Cube inspire awe, not just among other kids but also with adults.

Most of us have a Rubik's Cube at home or at least know somebody who has one. It has been, after all, one of the bestselling toys for decades. But how many of us can manage to solve it?

According to statistics, only 1 in 20 people who own a Rubik's Cube can claim to have solved it.

That's a pretty dismal figure, considering cubing is not all that tough. All that is required is a little patience, a keen desire to learn the process, and an easy-to-understand step-by-step guide penned by a young man who is as passionate about cubing as he is about helping others discover how to do it.

Harrington Yeh is a happy 10-year-old Rubik's Cube enthusiast from San Francisco who loves hockey, skiing, trap shooting, snowboarding, swimming, and traveling. He plays hockey for the San Francisco youth hockey team and even sings with the San Francisco Boys Chorus.

What's more, he loves playing the guitar and clarinet too. But his first love is CUBING (he has been cubing for years now)!

The genius kid learned how to solve the Rubik's Cube all on his own—a feat most adults fail to achieve. What started as a curiosity soon turned into a full-fledged passion, and the kid was hooked.

Harrington enjoys solving the cube so much that it has become his life's mission to help other kids learn it as well. And that is the reason he decided to put together this guide.

Through this book, you will not just learn how to solve the Rubik's Cube. You will discover how to do it in less than one minute (just like Harrington!) and in a super fun and exciting way.

Harrington's passion for cubing and his deep desire to teach other kids the skill he has mastered over time are evident in how he has penned this wonderfully detailed guide.

BENEFITS OF LEARNING HOW TO SOLVE THE RUBIK'S CUBE

According to the little Rubik's Cube expert, cubing brings so much more into your life than just the ability to impress your family and friends or get that minor ego boost when everyone exclaims what a rock star you are!

Cube Solving Teaches Patience

Let's admit this: Patience is not the most vital virtue for most people these days, including pre-teens. Make that, *especially* pre-teens.

Harrington realizes this (smart guy!) and therefore suggests both kids and adults start practicing cubing.

While this game can be exciting and fun once you get the hang of things, it can also seriously test your patience in the beginning.

The key is to keep persevering until you finally manage to solve it; the sense of accomplishment that you'll experience after that will be unmatched. (You may even experience a low-key feeling that you're the next Albert Einstein!)

Cube Solving Improves Your Memory

Among all the things that help improve your memory muscle, solving Rubik's Cube ranks pretty high up there. This is because you are required to practice cubing by using so many different algorithms.

Improving memory is particularly useful for students, who need enhanced memory to solve those math problems in their heads or better recall what the teacher has taught in school. And maybe also to remember that Mommy has asked them NOT to leave their wet towels on the bed!

Cube Solving Makes You Look Smart

There is absolutely no doubt about this one—cube-solving makes you look smart. And nerdy. And even like a genius.

Want to make your friends go "Wow!" at a birthday party? Bring your cube and unleash your inner cube expert. Want to render Aunt Jenny (who keeps bragging about how intelligent her son is) speechless? Impress her by solving the cube in under one minute!

Cube Solving Helps You Make Friends

Last but not the least, a speed-cubing kid is going to attract a lot of friends who will never miss an opportunity to brag about what a genius their friend is!

Cubing is also an excellent icebreaker; you can show your cubing moves to a random stranger on a subway, and there are bright chances they'll be impressed enough to be your next best friend for life!

SUMMARY

To sum up, learning how to solve the Rubik's Cube can be life changing. It is not just a fantastic way to spend your idle time; it also has the power to enhance your memory and self-esteem.

So, what are you waiting for? Get ready to learn how to solve the Rubik's Cube by waltzing your way through this easy-to-understand, fun guide.

And we promise it is not as tough as it seems!

1

FOR PARENTS – WHY EVERY KID NEEDS TO LEARN HOW TO SOLVE THE RUBIK'S CUBE

C ube solving comes with a multitude of benefits and keeping your child away from screens is just one of them.

In this modern age, most kids spend their spare time playing with gadgets, and they often struggle with a short attention span as a consequence. Solving the Rubik's Cube is a healthy hobby that can teach your children vital life lessons, along with keeping their ever-wavering minds busy.

From developing spatial awareness to teaching your little humans virtues like patience and perseverance, solving the Rubik's Cube promotes children's holistic development.

Introducing this amazing puzzle to your little ones can challenge their minds as it has for others for decades. The Rubik's cube is a great toy; not only is it inexpensive but no battery is required, and your kids can bring it everywhere with them. What more can you ask for?

If you're still not convinced, the below-listed benefits of learning how to solve the Cube will make you think again.

BRAIN ACTIVATION

When it comes to our brains (and maybe many other things too), the age-old adage rings true—*use it or lose it*. Brain activation is extremely crucial for kids in particular since it is a great way to sharpen the mind.

As a parent, we always want the best for our children—whether it is the clothes they wear, the school they go to, the toys they play with, or the food they eat. Why not encourage them to get involved in an activity that will boost their intelligence and force them to think logically!

Yes, we are talking about solving the Rubik's Cube here. You can view cube solving as a healthy brain exercise; it stimulates brain activity since it involves using a long list of algorithms to arrive at the desired result.

It is mentally stimulating for the child and extremely rewarding when the child finally manages to solve the Cube, irrespective of whether they achieve the feat independently or with the help of a book or online tutorial.

BETTER RETENTION POWER

Whether it is used in the classroom or on the playground, memory is one of the most basic learning foundations. Great memory or better retention power ensures your child does well in school and helps him/her score good grades.

Now, it is not that people are born with excellent memory skills. Rather, like most other skills, these can be developed with sustained practice.

Also, one of the biggest fears humans face as they age is the loss of memory. The good news is that scientists believe that if we continue to exercise our brains just like we do for the rest of our bodies, we can generally eliminate this fear from our lives.

Learning how to solve the Rubik's Cube is a great mental exercise that enhances memory and improves the brain's retention power. When solving the Cube, a child needs to put in hours of practice, which improves muscle memory.

So, if your child struggles with a short attention span or has trouble retaining one bit of information while doing something else, encouraging him/her to solve the Rubik's Cube might prove to be highly beneficial.

FINE MOTOR SKILLS DEVELOPMENT

There are scores of small muscles in our hands and wrists that we use daily to perform hundreds of tasks. Fine motor skills refer to the ability to make movements using these muscles. These skills start developing in children right from infanthood, and we rely heavily on them for doing small, basic jobs.

Whether it is buttoning up clothes, eating pasta using a fork, or pouring water into a glass, children are constantly employing their fine motor skills, and they continue to refine this throughout early childhood.

Solving the Rubik's Cube requires twisting it frequently, often quickly, which helps develop fine motor skills in children.

BETTER HAND-EYE COORDINATION

In addition to the development of fine motor skills, playing with the Rubik's Cube also involves the simultaneous use of eyes and hands, which improves hand-eye coordination in children.

Hand-eye coordination is a complex cognitive ability used to perform scores of tasks daily. It is of utmost importance for normal child development and also for academic success.

Cube solving is an activity that uses visual-spatial perception (simply put, whatever our eyes see) to guide our hands to take action accordingly. So, it enables children to use their eyes and hands to their optimum ability and in perfect unison.

IMPROVES REFLEXES

First and foremost, let us understand what reflexes are. Reflexes are nothing but involuntary responses that are not processed or controlled by the brain. For example, when a ball comes toward a tennis player, their reflex prompts them to hit it.

When you start speed-cubing (a term used for solving the Rubik's Cube quickly), it helps sharpen your reflexes. There are so many kids out there who can solve the Cube in a matter of seconds, which speaks volumes about their incredible brain functioning as well as their strong reflexes and quicker reaction time.

BUILDS FOCUS AND CONCENTRATION

The ability to concentrate varies from child to child, but most kids find it hard to focus on one thing completely. It even becomes tough to get them to finish their homework without getting too distracted!

We know that kids are inherently more energetic and active, but this should not be considered an excuse for their inability to concentrate for too long. If your child is suffering from poor concentration levels, introducing him/her to the mentally stimulating and highly engaging world of the Rubik's Cube may be a brilliant idea.

Unlike most other puzzles, Rubik's Cube is an open-ended puzzle with around 43 quintillion different ways of solving it. Another interesting fact about this toy is that there is no cheat code; everything you need to solve this puzzle is right in front of you. Also, every single move leads to a unique way of unscrambling the Cube.

So, it requires a certain level of focus and concentration for anyone to make progress in this game. As your child starts making small advances, their interest in the game will increase, and so will their level of concentration and focus.

ENHANCED FINGER DEXTERITY AND AGILITY

Kids continuously use their hands every minute of their waking time—from doing their homework to playing and giving high-fives! So, it is imperative that their hands, especially those tiny fingers, stay in great shape.

Playing with the Rubik's Cube is a great way to enhance finger dexterity and agility in both kids and adults.

Especially in speed-cubing, children need to twist the Cube in quick succession—multiple times in a small timeframe—making their fingers more agile. Finger dexterity and agility exercises can prove beneficial in the long run when kids are required to type fast or code quickly on their computers.

TEACHES PATIENCE

Ask any Cube lover and they will tell you how beautifully this puzzle tests their patience! Only people who are patient and resilient enough are eventually able to unscramble the Cube successfully.

Cube solving involves keeping track of multiple moves in a step-by-step fashion. The entire process has a particular sequence that needs to be performed with utmost concentration, requiring tremendous patience.

Even if your children learn some algorithms from a YouTube tutorial or a book, breaking these into simple steps and then applying those steps, each of which builds on the last, is extremely mentally stimulating and engaging. It also requires a high level of patience.

PROMOTES MINDFULNESS

Mindfulness is the new buzzword these days, isn't it? From corporate executives to A-list celebrities and health experts, everyone is talking about how important it is to incorporate a little bit of mindfulness into our daily routines.

Now, simply put, mindfulness is the art of being mentally aware and focusing completely on the *present*—something that a person solving the Rubik's Cube already does!

Learning to solve the Rubik's cube can be such a beautiful way of teaching mindfulness to young children, whose monkey minds keep jumping from one thought to another. When kids learn to give their undivided attention to one task (solving the Cube, in this case), they learn the basics of mindfulness.

SUMMARY

Solving the Rubik's Cube is a fantastic way of keeping young kids' brains active, sharpening their mental reflexes, and improving their problem-solving skills.

An important thing to note here is that all of the skills mentioned above are already present in children; the only requirement is to polish them to a level where they start shining brightly, and this is where the Rubik's Cube comes in!

Also, the sense of accomplishment that solving this puzzle would award your kids will be worth every second they spend on learning the tricks.

Now you understand that playing with Rubik's Cube will not only make your little ones smarter but will also teach them patience and mindfulness. We will let Harrington take over from here to introduce your children to the history of this legendary toy named the Rubik's Cube.

2

HISTORY OF THE RUBIK'S CUBE

Hello Friends! I am Harrington Yeh, and I am here to share my passion for cubing with all of you! I have been cubing for quite a few years now and would love to teach you all my secrets and tricks for solving the Rubik's Cube; also, to get you to experience how fun and exciting this puzzle is.

But before we move on to the process of solving the cube and then learning some tips and tricks of speedcubing, let us first learn about the history of this terrific puzzle, which has earned the label of the best-selling toy of all time. (Quite an achievement, isn't it?)

THE INVENTION OF THE RUBIK'S CUBE

The massively popular Rubik's Cube is the brainchild of a Hungarian architect and sculptor named Ernő Rubik. He once taught interior design at the Academy of Applied Arts and Crafts in Budapest. He found himself struggling with finding a perfect way to help his students understand 3-D movement.

It was almost half a century ago, in 1974 when Rubik was just a 29-year-old guy determined to create a structural design problem for his students. He spent months toying around with different blocks of cubes—trying to hold them together with adhesive, rubber bands, and even paper clips.

He made these cubes out of wood or paper and continued trying to assemble them in a way in which each block of the cube could move independently without the entire structure falling apart. (He wanted to teach the basics of 3-D movement to his students, remember?)

Rubik finally did manage to create "The Cube," but little did he know at the time that the masterpiece he had created would earn accolades *not* as a teaching tool but as a super-exciting puzzle that would keep young minds hooked for generations to come.

This cube was made almost entirely out of wood and was pretty huge, and he had to cut down the corners because of its large size. Each of the six faces of the cube has nine square pieces in a

3 x 3 pattern. There were six solid colors shortlisted for each of the six sides—red, green, blue, orange, yellow, and white.

But what is fascinating is that Rubik himself could not solve the puzzle he had just created! Interestingly, I found this fact in Rubik's own words in an article titled "Rubik's Cube – PuzzleSolver" (accessed April 8, 2021 at http://www. puzzlesolver.com/puzzle.php?id=29;page=15):

"It was wonderful to see how, after only a few turns, the colors became mixed, apparently in a random fashion. It was tremendously satisfying to watch this color parade. After a nice walk when you have seen many lovely sights, you decide to go home; after a while I decided it was time to go home, let us put the cubes back in order. And it was at that moment that I came face to face with the Big Challenge: What is the way home?"

Although the cube looked deceptively simple at first glance, Rubik had no idea how to solve it, let alone to do it quickly. It took him a little less than a month to restore the puzzle that he had created!

Rubik confesses that, initially, he believed it would take him an eternity to solve the cube just by randomly twisting it. Soon, he figured out that he needed to learn a sequence of movements for rearranging the small cubes (or pieces, as they are known) to solve the puzzle.

After almost a month of perseverance and trying out different permutations, the man finally solved the Cube. Even after practicing regularly, it still took Rubik up to one minute to solve it. (Modern-day speedcubers would probably scoff at that!) But this marked the beginning of his and his iconic puzzle's awe-inspiring journey.

Some Interesting Facts:

- Rubik initially called his puzzle the Magic Cube. The name Rubik's Cube came much later.
- He prefers to call the Rubik's Cube his *discovery* rather than *invention,* as the puzzle theoretically existed before he'd created it.
- Rubik initially believed that his puzzle would appeal only to people with a keen interest in science, math, or engineering. He claims that it is shocking for him to see people from all backgrounds getting attracted to the Cube.

PATENTING THE "MAGIC CUBE"

On the 30th of January 1975, Rubik applied for a patent for his "Magic Cube." In his application to the Patent Office in

Hungary, he called his creation a "spatial logic toy" and not a puzzle.

At that time, puzzles weren't all that popular in the country and were available only at some souvenir shops. And since Hungary was a communist-controlled country back then, even the toy production was not too high.

Now, here was a puzzle that was *also* a toy. This concept was so novel that it caught the fancy of a small toy-making cooperative in Budapest.

Rubik got the patent in early 1977, and the first Magic Cubes appeared in toy stores in Budapest later that year. These cubes could not be easily pulled apart, as interlocking pieces of plastic firmly held them together—ideal for kids' toys.

At around the same time, two other people in different parts of the world were also applying for similar patents. A Japanese national named Terutoshi Ishigi, a self-taught engineer and business owner, also applied for a patent for an almost identical Magic Cube mechanism. An American named Larry Nichols managed to get a patent *before* Rubik for a cube held together by magnets.

However, Nichols' cube did not impress toy manufacturers (apparently using magnets to hold the cube together wasn't such a great idea after all!) and was rejected by almost all of them. One of these was the Ideal Toy Corporation, the company that went on to buy the rights to the Rubik's Cube and make it a household name in the 1980s.

THE RUBIK'S CUBE STARTS TRAVELING WORLDWIDE

Although the Magic Cube launched toward the end of 1977, the sales were not very promising during the initial few years. However, things changed for the better once Hungarian businessman Tibor Laczi spotted the toy.

As it turned out, the gentleman was enjoying his coffee at a restaurant when he noticed one of the waiters toying with the Cube. Being an amateur mathematician himself, Laczi was hooked. The puzzle impressed him so much that the very next day he asked for permission to sell the Magic Cube in the West.

It is reported that when Laczi first met Ernő Rubik, the latter's shabby clothes and disheveled appearance shocked him. He immediately understood that even though the man struggled financially, he was a genius to have created such an amazing puzzle.

He even assured Rubik that his creation would sell millions worldwide, a prophecy that came out to be true—and HOW!

The Magic Cube tasted success for the first time when Laczi decided to demonstrate it at the Nuremberg toy fair. An interesting thing to note here is that he did not *officially* exhibit the toy but instead just casually walked around the fair playing with it.

He managed to attract the attention of Tom Kremer, a British toy expert. Like Laczi, Kremer was also super impressed with the Cube, and so he secured an order of one million pieces with a major toy corporation, Ideal Toy, to release the toy worldwide.

THE RUBIK'S CUBE FINALLY GETS ITS NAME AND WINS THE WORLD OVER

When Ideal Toy Company decided to distribute the Magic Cube worldwide, they needed a recognizable name to trademark, so they renamed it as the Rubik's Cube to credit its inventor. (Or should we say, discoverer?)

In 1980, Ideal Toy Company launched the Rubik's cube globally, and the rest, as they say, is history!

An all-new Rubik's Cube was introduced in the West in a slightly different form due to safety concerns and packaging regulations. The newer version was much lighter, which made solve times much quicker.

Initially, sales were pretty modest. By the middle of 1980, the Ideal Toy Company launched an advertising campaign on TV and in newspapers, which played a huge role in popularizing the Cube.

By the end of the year, Rubik's Cube won the UK Toy of the Year award and similar best toy awards in Germany, France, and the U.S. *The Rubik's Cube's awe-inspiring story of success had finally begun!*

By 1981 the toy had become a huge craze across the globe. In the first three years of its worldwide launch, the total sales was a whopping 100 million units. You realize the popularity of the Rubik's Cube when you see that it started appearing on the front page of world-renowned magazines and newspapers.

The *Washington Post* called it "a puzzle that's moving like fast food right now," while *New Scientist* carried a report that claimed the Cube had "captivated the attention of children of ages from 7 to 70 all over the world this summer."

In March that year, a speedcubing competition was held in Munich by none other than the *Guinness Book of World Records*!

And in 1982, the very first Rubik's Cube World Championship was organized in Budapest, in which 20 competitors from different parts of the world came together with a single mission —to solve the Cube as fast as possible.

A 16-year-old American from Los Angeles, Minh Thai, was the championship winner. Minh solved the Cube in 22.95 seconds in the FIRST ever speedcubing championship. Rumor has it that the unofficial speed records could have been 10 seconds or even less at the time.

Minh Thai even went on to publish a book titled *The Winning Solution*, in which he taught other cube enthusiasts how to solve the puzzle.

Rubik's Cube fever had caught on so well that people spent hours figuring out the solution to the puzzle. And as people's obsession with the Cube grew, so did its notoriety of being unsolvable.

Around this time, a 12-year-old boy named Patrick Bossert released a book titled *You Can Do the Cube*, which became so popular among people eager to learn the tricks to solving the Cube that it went on to sell 1.5 million copies worldwide.

So, this pretty much proves that once you get addicted to this extraordinary toy, you just HAVE to figure out a way to unscramble it. (This is why you are here, right?)

WAS THE RUBIK'S CUBE SUCCESS SHORT-LIVED?

After taking the world by storm from 1980 to 1983, the Cube's popularity started fading as its novelty factor receded. Sales also started dropping as a result, and in late 1982, the *New York Times* reported that "the [Rubik's Cube] craze had died," and the paper even went on to call it a "fad."

However, the Cube continued to sell well in countries like China and the USSR, where it was introduced later and was in short supply.

Now, does this mean that the success of the Rubik's Cube was short-lived?

Well, not really!

All through the 1980s and 1990s, Rubik's Cube had respectable global demand and sales. While the sales weren't as spectacular as its first introduction, they were decent nevertheless.

The most important thing is that Rubik's Cube made Ernő Rubik the first self-made millionaire in communist Hungary. He was inspiring thousands of people, both young and old, to form clubs to play and study solutions to the puzzle.

Known as "Cubic Rubes," Rubik's Cube enthusiasts continued to hold unofficial competitions to solve the Cube in the least amount of time.

WHY DID THE CUBE LOSE ITS POPULARITY?

Now we already know that during the Cube's worldwide launch it became a massive hit. You can easily compare the popularity of Rubik's Cube in the early 1980s to say... the Avengers. (Yes, it was THAT popular!)

This massive popularity is why Rubik's Cube is still known as the best-selling toy in history.

But then, in the late 1980s and 1990s, the Cube somehow fell out of fashion, and sales started plummeting. Many tabloids and newspapers were quick to write it off as another fad. One of the reasons behind its loss of popularity could be that most people found it too hard to solve and probably just gave up.

The Cube didn't come with an instruction manual that would teach people how to solve it, and it wasn't possible to look up solutions on the internet like we do today. Thank God for all the YouTube tutorials! People put away in drawers this once popular toy out of frustration until internet usage revived it.

CUBE REVIVAL

Remember we talked about the world's first Rubik's Cube World Championship held in Budapest in 1982? Yes, the same one where American teenager Minh Thai won.

In that competition, among the 20 competitors was a 17-year-old woman named Jessica Fridrich. She was the only woman participant and represented her country, Czechoslovakia, at the championship.

Now, while most of the world got tired of trying to solve the Cube in a few years after that world championship, Fridrich's love affair with the toy continued unabated. The young woman did not just love to solve the Cube; she practiced several hours a day, trying to develop faster ways to finish it.

Her passion for the Rubik's Cube continued for years, and after a while, she came up with a pretty impressive and relatively simple system of solving it.

In 1997, almost a decade after she'd come up with that "method," Fridrich decided to put it up on the internet (yes, the internet had arrived by then) just for fun. Since cubing was not at all mainstream at that time, she never expected anyone to check out what she had uploaded or try to learn algorithms.

However, time proved her wrong!

By 2000, Fridrich realized how popular her page had become. There were hundreds of people who visited the page to understand her method of solving the Cube.

And once fans started sharing their solving strategies on internet video sites like YouTube, there was no looking back. In 2008, the annual sales of Rubik's Cube crossed the 15 million mark.

So, in a way, the Internet managed to "revive" the Rubik's Cube.

THE INTERNET MAKES THE CUBE POPULAR AGAIN

As more and more people started getting online, it gradually increased the Cube's popularity, as cubers were now able to post their email addresses along with their solve times online on a CD-ROM titled *Rubik's Games*.

A Yahoo group soon came along called Speedsolving the Rubik's Cube; it invited cubers to share their tips and tricks.

In 2000, a man named Ron van Bruchem started an online forum called speedcubing.com. Ron van Bruchem was one of the hundreds of thousands of Rubik's Cube fans from the 1980s who lost interest in the puzzle once the initial craze subsided. But when the Cube started gaining popularity again via the Internet, van Bruchem's love for the puzzle also revived, and so he created the forum.

Gradually, the online cubing community began to grow, and talks of holding a global championship like the one held decades back in 1982 started gathering steam.

A world championship was held in 2003 in Toronto, Canada. Still, it did not turn out to be a success due to several reasons— no detailed regulations, no time limit, too many competitors, and some unfair decisions, to name a few.

Anyway, what is important is that this championship managed to turn speedcubing into an organized sport and led to the birth of the World Cube Association.

Today, almost 20,000 cubers compete in various competitions across the world. The World Cube Association itself holds close to 700 competitions every year, in which mostly teenagers compete with each other.

The number of competitions proves that despite the availability of high-tech toys and gadgets, this old-school, analog puzzle, which can easily fit into a pocket and does not need any battery to run, continues to attract thousands of young people (myself included)!

If you need any further proof of this toy's fantastic popularity, consider this: As of 2018, total sales are more than 350 million units of the Rubik's Cube worldwide.

Need I say more?

IMPORTANT MILESTONES IN THE RUBIK'S CUBE'S INCREDIBLE JOURNEY

Now that we are aware of the interesting ups and downs that the Cube endured since it came into existence in 1974, let us quickly recount all the important milestones in its incredible journey:

- In 1974, Hungarian Professor of Interior Design Ernő Rubik created the first-ever Rubik's Cube as a teaching tool to help his students understand 3-D problems.
- The man who created the cube himself could not solve it initially. It took Ernő Rubik almost a month to solve the puzzle.
- Rubik called his creation the "Magic Cube" and applied for a patent on January 30, 1975.
- The patent finally came along in early 1977. A Budapest toy store launched the first Magic Cubes.
- Hungarian businessman Tibor Laczi spotted the Magic Cube at a restaurant and decided to take it to one of the biggest toy fairs at the time—the Nuremberg toy fair.
- At the fair, Magic Cube impressed Tom Kremer, a British toy expert, who then entered into a deal with the U.S. toy corporation Ideal Toy to launch the puzzle worldwide in 1980.
- Ideal Toy renamed the Magic Cube as Rubik's Cube to credit its inventor and because they didn't like that the name made it sound as if the cube had something to do with witchcraft.
- Following an advertising campaign by Ideal Toy Company, sales of the Rubik's Cube skyrocketed; it sold 100 million units in the first three years of its launch.
- In 1982, the first Rubik's Cube World Championship

was organized in Budapest, which American teenager Minh Thai won.

- The late 1980s and 1990s witnessed a serious fall in the popularity of the Rubik's Cube.
- In 1997, cubing enthusiast Jessica Fridrich uploaded onto the internet an impressive and relatively simple system of solving the Cube.
- Soon, her page became popular among other cubers trying to learn how to solve the cube quickly.
- The internet once again popularized the Cube; cubers started posting their solve times and sharing their solving strategies on YouTube sites.
- In 2004, the World Cube Association was established, and today it holds close to 700 competitions every year.

3

FUN FACTS ABOUT THE RUBIK'S CUBE

D id you enjoy learning about the interesting history of the Rubik's Cube? If yes, you're going to love this chapter even more!

As you know by now, Rubik's Cube is a puzzle that has challenged the minds of thousands of people since its launch. One of the reasons behind its tremendous popularity and success is that it is kind of addictive; once you've experienced the thrill of solving the Cube, you just can't keep yourself from coming back for more!

As a tribute to this insanely popular, brain-challenging, and twisty-turn colorful toy, I have compiled a list of some amazing Rubik's Cube fun facts that I'm sure you'll find super interesting:

FUN FACTS ABOUT THE RUBIK'S CUBE'S STRUCTURE

- The standard 3 x 3 Rubik's Cube is a six-sided puzzle with nine pieces on each side in six different solid colors—red, blue, green, yellow, orange, and white. It combines 26 small cubes, called "pieces" or "cubelets," and 54 outer surfaces.
- Each of the tiny cubes forming the Rubik's Cube can be twisted and rotated along the rows and faces. In the end, the cuber's main goal is to ensure that all the pieces on each side of the cube are the same color.
- Although the standard Rubik's Cube has a 3 x 3 configuration, it can come in 2 x 2 or 4 x 4 and even more complicated versions.

FUN FACTS ABOUT THE 22 X 22 CUBE

- Coreen Puzzle created this 22 x 22 cube, and they hold the world record for building the largest cube-based puzzle EVER.
- This mind-blowing (like literally!) puzzle has 484 colored squares on each of its faces, along with 2691 functioning parts.
- Do you wish to know how many possible ways to solve this cube? Well, it's 4.3 x 10^1795 different ways. That

number is so *huge* that there is not even a proper name for it!

- An impressive fact about this custom-made Cube is that it almost completely wore out a consumer-grade 3D printer.
- If this Cube gets scrambled into a rainbow mess, no one can begin to guess how many lifetimes it would take for even the smartest of Rubik's Cube experts to unscramble it completely.

FUN FACTS ABOUT THE WORLD'S LARGEST RUBIK'S CUBE (IN TERMS OF SIZE)

- British puzzle maker Tony Fisher has created the world's largest Rubik's Cube in Ipswich, UK.
- This masterpiece measured 2.022 meters x 2.022 meters x 2.022 meters, and it was unveiled on November 18, 2019.
- It looks exactly like the standard 3 x 3 Rubik's Cube, and its layers also move exactly in the same manner as a regular Cube does.
- It took Tony a total time of 330 hours to build this humongous Cube.
- Tony had previously also set a world record by creating the world's largest Rubik's Cube in 2016 that measured 1.57 meters on each side. However, having

had his record broken in 2018, he was motivated to
build this massive Cube.

- Building the world's largest Cube wasn't exactly cheap;
  it cost Tony almost 2,000 pounds to create this
  structure.

FUN FACTS ABOUT THE WORLD'S COSTLIEST RUBIK'S CUBE

- While an ordinary Rubik's Cube does not cost much
  (you can get one for less than $5 online) if you love the
  game a tad too much and if you have too much money
  to flaunt, you can go for the world's most expensive
  Rubik's Cube (the Masterpiece Rubik's Cube); it will
  make your poorer by $2.5 million.
- Despite its exorbitant price tag, this *toy* is fully
  functional, which means you can twist and turn it all
  you want.
- This masterpiece has been made using 18-carat gold and
  has 25 gems instead of the regular "pieces." These gems
  include 185-carats of diamonds, amethysts, emeralds,
  and rubies. (That explains the outrageous price.)
- The Masterpiece Rubik's Cube was created in 1995 by
  Diamond Cutters International to commemorate the
  15th anniversary of the Rubik's Cube attaining
  international popularity.

FUN FACTS ABOUT DIFFERENT TYPES OF RUBIK'S CUBES

- From the Pentamix to the Mirror Cube, there are so many interesting variants of the standard 3 x 3 Rubik's Cube that it can be truly mindboggling.
- Pentamix is regarded as one of the toughest Rubik's Cubes to solve. It looks spectacular and comprises 975 individual parts and over 1,200 pieces.
- Even if you consider yourself a Rubik's Cube pro, a single glance at the uncompleted Mirror Cube is enough to send your mind into a tizzy! This puzzle does not have any colored pieces; instead, it's made up of various pieces (not all are cubes) of different sizes.
- If you know someone who has mastered the 3 x 3 Rubik's Cube, you can give them the Ghost Cube. This one is a shape-shifting Cube, so the person will probably have a hard time wrapping their head around the fact that it needs to be solved not by color but by shape.
- Its name may surprise you, but yes, there is a thing called the Idiot's Cube. It looks exactly like the standard 3 x 3 Rubik's Cube, only there are no colorful pieces on *any* of the sides. So, long story short, being able to solve this Cube is, well, *impossible*. The next time you feel you're suffering from low self-esteem, just get this

Cube and solve it, or maybe just *pretend* you've solved it!

- If you thought it couldn't get any more bizarre than this, there is even a thing called the Braillecube. You got it right—this one for the visually impaired. It is as if someone thought, *Why should the visually impaired be spared the frustration of trying to solve the Rubik's Cube?* and came up with one for them too!

FUN FACTS ABOUT SOLVING THE RUBIK'S CUBE

- There are more than 43 quintillion different configurations to solve it (43,252,003,274,489,856,000, to be precise)! If you had that kind of money ($43 quintillion), it would last you for the next 118,000 years if you spent $1 trillion every single day!
- If you twist the Rubik's Cube once every second, it will take you 1.4 trillion years to go through all the possible configurations. Even if you started at the Big Bang, you would still be solving the Cube at present!
- Despite the seemingly endless number of combinations to solve the puzzle, it is possible to solve every single Cube position in twenty or fewer moves.
- And despite the startlingly large number of people who've been fascinated by the Rubik's Cube, less than 5.8% of the global population can claim to have solved

it. Most just toyed with it for a while and gave up after not being able to figure out how to solve it.

FUN FACTS ABOUT THE POPULARITY OF RUBIK'S CUBE

- Rubik's Cube is the best-selling toy in history, but its inventor, Ernő Rubik, prefers to call it a "piece of art" rather than a mere "toy." And considering how much artwork this puzzle has inspired, I can't help but agree with Mr. Rubik!

- In the last four decades, total sales have reached more than 350 million Rubik's Cubes worldwide. To understand this better, let us assume that each Cube costs $10. In that case, the world has spent $3.5 billion on this puzzle alone!

- We learned in the previous chapter that the Rubik's Cube debuted in 1974. By the mid-1980s, almost one-fifth of the world's population had played with this toy at least once!

- Patrick Bossert's bestselling book *You Can Do the Cube*, published in 1981, was originally meant only for his friends who were desperate to learn how to solve the puzzle. One of these friends was the son of an editor at Penguin Books, so that is how the book finally got published. Just to remind you, it sold over 1.5 million copies worldwide!

- Rubik's Cube won the Toy of the Year Award in 1980 and 1981.

- Saturday mornings for many kids in the 1980s began with a bowl of cereal and watching an animated series on ABC network based on their favorite toy, the Rubik's Cube! Named *Rubik, the Amazing Cube*, it aired 13 episodes in which the toy had a personality complete with a face, legs, and magical powers.

- In 1981, a British pop group named The Barron Knights released a song, called *Mr. Rubik*, about a man who went crazy after playing with a Rubik's Cube! The song appeared on their album *Twisting The Knights Away*.

- Rubik's Cube managed to enter the Oxford English Dictionary in 1982.

- New York's famous Museum of Modern Art has a permanent Rubik's Cube exhibit.

- More than 40,000 videos on YouTube alone teach different tips and tricks for solving the Rubik's Cube.

- To honor the 40th anniversary of the Rubik's Cube in 2014, the Liberty Science Center (LSC) in Jersey City hosted a $5 million, media-rich exhibition "Beyond Rubik's Cube" with lead creative partner Google and the Cube's inventor, Ernő Rubik.

- In this one-of-a-kind exhibition, a 26-foot tall, illuminated Cube, hanging in the LSC atrium, greeted the guests. Cube-solving robots and a giant walk-in

Cube that showed the puzzle's inner workings were some other attractions at the exhibition.

- On April 26, 2014, the Bank of America Tower (1 Bryant Park) and the Conde Nast Building (4 Times Square) were lit in Rubik's Cube colors to mark the world's bestselling toy's 40th anniversary. Even the Empire State Building followed suit on May 8, 2014!

- Google created an interactive doodle of the Rubik's Cube on May 19, 2014, to celebrate the 40th anniversary of its creation. The doodle allowed the users to twist and turn parts of the Cube to solve it, and it even allowed them to keep a score of their moves on the side.

- Rubik's Cube is quite the rock star as it got featured in quite a few Hollywood movies. Some of these include *Interstellar, Hellboy, The Amazing Spider-Man, The Machinist, Let Me In, Armageddon, Little Big Shots, The Wedding Singer, Let The Right One, Brick*, and *Mr. Peabody and Sherman*. Phew! That's quite a lot of movies, isn't it?

- Even popular television series like *Seinfeld, Lucifer,* and *The Simpsons* had sequences that featured the Rubik's Cube.

- And probably the final pop-culture push to the Rubik's Cube's popularity in the 2000s came from none other than Hollywood actor Will Smith. He was solving the Cube to impress a potential business associate in the movie *The Pursuit of Happyness*. This scene was part of the trailer, which added to the popularity of the Cube.

- The hugely popular American sitcom *The Big Bang Theory* also featured a tissue box that resembled a Rubik's Cube (understandable since the series revolved around many socially awkward but brilliant people).

FUN FACTS ABOUT RUBIK'S CUBE AS AN EXPRESSION OF ART

- Not appropriate only for the entertainment industry, this humble toy called the Rubik's Cube has also motivated several artists to create art inspired by it. From captivating street art to amazing portraits and art installations, Rubik's Cube has been the inspiration behind many fascinating works of art.
- In 2003, Disney Pop Century Resort opened a huge Rubik's Cube installation with a staircase.
- Toronto-based Cube Works Studio created a massive 200-foot long, 13-foot-tall Guinness World Record-breaking mosaic of the Macau skyline using more than 85,000 Rubik's Cubes. It is probably the world's biggest Rubik's Cube mosaic art and took several months to finish.
- Many artists like Giovanni Contardi from Italy are making thousands of dollars by turning hundreds of

Rubik's Cubes into huge celebrity portraits. And let me tell you, each of them looks stunning!

- The *art* of creating *art* using Rubik's Cubes even has a name – Rubik's Cubism!

FUN FACTS ABOUT SPEEDCUBING

- Speedcubing refers to solving the Cube as quickly as possible, and any person who competes in speedcubing competitions is called a speedcuber.
- The World Cube Association (WCA) organizes World Championships wherein speedcubers worldwide come together to participate.
- These championships take place every other year, and the last one was in Melbourne, Australia from the 11th to 14th of July 2019.
- Interestingly, speedcubers who participate in these tournaments do not use the Rubik's Cube *exclusively*. Several other companies have cropped up that make similar cubes but with better technology that allows for faster solving times.
- Speedcubing is not just a sport or hobby, but a global business too.
- The WCA allows speedcubers to lubricate their cubes so that they can be twisted and turned quickly, easily, and more reliably compared to the non-lubricated

cubes. And there is even a list of lubricants that the cubers are allowed to use.

- Most speedcubing competitions use a trimmed mean of five formats. The competitor will do five solves, eliminate the fastest and slowest, then the mean of the remaining three will be their scores.

- Yusheng Du from China is the current record holder for the fastest solved Cube—3.47 seconds, beating Australian speedcuber Feliks Zemdegs by 0.75 seconds.

SOME BIZARRE RUBIK'S CUBE WORLD RECORDS

While the above-listed speedcubing record is super inspiring, several other Rubik's Cube world records come across as pretty bizarre. For instance, did you know that Rubik's Cube can be solved while free-falling from a plane or that people are trying to solve the Cube underwater?

Here is a list of some bizarre Rubik's Cube world records that will make your jaw drop:

- When it comes to solving the Rubik's Cube, there are plenty of records with different variations, but this one is downright bizarre! There is a record for solving the Rubik's Cube while falling from an airplane. Yes, you read that right! The record-holder is a man named Dan

Knight, who managed to solve the Cube in under 35 seconds—just 10 seconds before his parachute opened!

- Do you know who the youngest person ever to solve the Rubik's Cube is? She is a Chinese toddler named Ruxin Liu who managed to solve the Cube in a little over 1.5 hours at the Weifang Open held on April 14, 2013. She was merely three years plus 118 days old at that time. When I was that age, I was probably eating sand!

- As if solving the Cube with open eyes wasn't challenging enough, some geniuses are attempting to solve the puzzle blindfolded, relying solely on their memory! According to the rules of these Blindfolded Rubik's Cube competitions, players have just 10 seconds to memorize the Cube. Then they have to solve it blindfolded based on whatever they can remember. The current world record of speedsolving the standard 3 x 3 Rubik's Cube while blindfolded is Max Hilliard from the U.S., who managed to do it in just 15.50 seconds at the Cubing USA Nationals 2019 held in Baltimore in August 2019.

- A huge percentage of the world population finds it ultra-difficult to solve the Rubik's Cube with their hands. But some people take only a few seconds to solve the Cube with their *feet*! Mohammed Aiman Koli from India holds the current world record for speed-solving the standard 3 x 3 Rubik's Cube using the feet, and he achieved it in 15.56 seconds at the VJTI Mumbai Cube Open 2019 in Mumbai on 27 December 2019. It is interesting to note here that many speedcubers find the concept of solving the Cube using feet kind of cringeworthy.

- Another Indian, Illayaram Sekar, holds the world record for solving the maximum number of Rubik's Cubes *underwater. Without taking any breaks.* He took a total of two minutes and seventeen seconds to solve six Cubes underwater. Are you also wondering, like me, how he managed to hold his breath for so long?

- There are a few speedcubers who can solve the Cube using *just one hand.* One such speedcuber known for one-handed speed solving is an American named Anthony Michael Brooks. He even starred in a Volkswagen commercial called "You Can't Fake Fast."

- Are you thinking it can't get more bizarre than this? Wait, there is more! Did you know that there is even a record for the fastest robot to solve the Rubik's Cube? This record is held by "Sub1 Reloaded," a robot made by Albert Beer from Germany, which managed to solve the Cube in 0.637 seconds!

- Rubik's Cubes have even been solved in space and on top of Mount Everest!

- When it comes to the most *unbelievable* of Rubik's Cube records, it would be unfair not to mention Que

Jianyu, a Chinese teenager. The 13-year-old is regarded as the Master of Rubik's Cubes. And rightly so, since he is the fastest speedcuber to solve three Rubik's Cubes using both hands and feet simultaneously! Not just that, he also broke the record for the fastest time to solve a Rubik's Cube while hanging upside down. And the boy can solve three Rubik's Cubes in a little over five minutes ... *while juggling them*!

SUMMARY

After reading all this amazing and awe-inspiring stuff about the Rubik's Cube (and how people are still totally crazy about it), I'm sure you'd also agree with Ernő Rubik—perhaps it *would* be unfair to call the Cube just a toy or a puzzle. It is certainly a piece of art that has kept people enchanted for over four and a half decades!

I know by now all of you are getting super excited to learn how to solve this piece of art, but before that, you *must* know *why* you want to learn it in the first place.

4

WHY SHOULD YOU BE SOLVING THE RUBIK'S CUBE?

Are you still asking yourself this question?

Well, a *simple* answer to that can be because the world is still hooked on it, even though it is so hard to solve, even though it is an old-school puzzle, and even though there are more than 43 quintillion ways of solving it!

However, as you must know by now, I do not prefer simple. (I solved the Rubik's Cube all by myself, after all!)

You should learn how to solve the Rubik's Cube because of ALL of the below-mentioned reasons:

IT TEACHES YOU PERSEVERANCE

Back when the Rubik's Cube was launched worldwide, it made people go crazy (as we discussed in detail in the last chapter). However, as any of you who has ever held it in your hands already knows, solving the Cube is no walk in the park. It requires a level of grit and determination that few possess, and since back in those days there were no online tutorials or any set rules of solving the puzzle, people started giving up.

Even in this age and time, when you can find dozens of step-by-step tutorials on YouTube, solving the Cube is not an easy task. Talking from experience here.

When I first got attracted to the Rubik's Cube, I thought that I'd be able to solve it with online tutorials (it looked deceptively simple to me at the time, and I had already figured out how to solve one side all by myself).

However, a few minutes into my first video, I couldn't understand a thing. I tried some other videos, but none of them helped much. That's when I decided I'd do it on my own. And I'll be honest—it took time; lots of it.

There were times when I was almost moved to tears. There were times when I felt like giving up. At times, my mom got a little concerned because I spent way too much time with my Rubik's Cube.

But my determination to solve the puzzle all by myself kept me going, and one fine day I finally held an unscrambled cube in my hand. The sheer joy that I experienced at the moment was immeasurable. I felt as if I'd conquered the world!

So, friends, the first and probably the most important thing that solving the Rubik's Cube will teach you is perseverance—a skill that will help you excel in every sphere of life.

IT HELPS IN THE DEVELOPMENT OF STEM SKILLS

In case any of you are wondering, STEM skills are the skills required in the fields of Science, Technology, Engineering, and Mathematics.

Since solving the Cube requires understanding and learning different algorithms, you can get smarter in all of the fields mentioned above. It generally requires you to think critically and then formulate your strategies to solve the puzzle.

So, it teaches you the basic STEM skills and develops your critical thinking that enhances those skills.

And it is not just me. Even Patrick Bossert (remember the kid who wrote the bestselling book on solving the Cube in 1981?) agrees. He credits his love for solving the Rubik's Cube for stimulating his logical reasoning skills.

So, if you have any doubts in your mind as to whether you have it in you to become a successful computer programmer, engineer, or just some random science guy, solving the Cube will answer that for you.

IT IMPROVES YOUR CONCENTRATION LEVEL

My mom says it is a challenge for her to get me to sit in one place for any amount of time. But not when I'm playing with my Rubik's Cube!

We, as kids, are naturally curious and full of energy, which kind of explains why we are so keen to jump from one task to another. We just get bored so easily! Especially, when we are required to do stuff that is not *interesting* enough—like cleaning our cupboards, helping with the dishes, or even studying—we tend to lose focus.

Also, frequent exposure to our gadgets' flashing screens makes it difficult to concentrate on one task for too long.

The plain old Rubik's Cube can come to our rescue. When playing with the Cube, you tend to get so absorbed in solving the puzzle that nothing else matters. It activates your brain cells and greatly enhances your concentration levels.

IT IMPROVES PROBLEM-SOLVING SKILLS

What exactly is the Cube? It is a *problem* that needs to be *solved*, isn't it? Needing full concentration and focus, it forces you to divide a bigger problem into smaller tasks and then tackle each, one by one.

Cube solving fully engages your brain and greatly enhances your problem-solving skills. Let me explain this with the help of a simple example.

When you are solving the Cube, you have to counter a lot of conditional algorithms. Like, if I twist this side up, then the red square will be next to the blue one. Or if I twist this other side up, then I will get two green squares side by side.

These algorithms hone your problem-solving skills and make you so much smarter in the process, bringing us to our next point.

IT MAKES YOU LOOK SMART

Okay, there is absolutely no doubt about this one! Most people look fascinated when you show them how to solve the Rubik's Cube. And if you show off your speedcubing skills, they might just think you're a genius!

The reason behind this is that it takes a certain level of commitment, patience, and, of course, brainpower to solve the

Cube—something that many people are just not interested enough to put in. So, when they come across someone who has managed to do all of that, they feel impressed.

I know for a fact that a lot of my friends got hooked onto the Cube after watching me solve it easily.

Now let me tell you that it is, indeed, a struggle initially; especially if you do not have anyone to guide you. (Most online tutorials are super confusing!) But with continuous practice and a keen interest in puzzle-solving, you should be able to do it.

I know. I did. So come on—it can't be *that* tough!

But yes, in the eyes of those who have no clue how to solve it, you will be no less than Einstein!

IT IS AN EXCELLENT WAY TO PASS TIME

If you think about it carefully, there are so many moments in a day when you're doing absolutely nothing. For example, when you're waiting for your school bus or dinner.

Instead of wasting away that time, why not just take out your Rubik's Cube and start playing? Its small size and the fact that it is an analog toy make it so convenient for you to take along wherever you go.

So, the next time Mommy gives you a time-out, don't forget to sneak in your Rubik's Cube to keep yourself entertained throughout. (Don't tell her I gave you this idea!)

SUMMARY

To sum up this chapter, we can say that solving the Rubik's Cube makes you smarter in so many more ways than you can imagine.

And don't forget, smart people run the world!

Also, the immeasurable satisfaction and the sense of accomplishment you experience when holding a solved Cube in your hands make every second that you put into it worthwhile. You know that feeling a superhero gets after saving the planet from a deadly alien attack? *That's* precisely how you feel when you solve the Cube for the first time. (I am talking from personal experience here!)

Now that we have already talked about this super awesome puzzle's history and the numerous benefits of solving it, let us move on to the *real* deal.

In the next few chapters, I will teach you how to solve the Rubik's Cube in the simplest way possible. I hope that you enjoy this journey as much as I did. Have loads of fun throughout, and please, on days you feel like giving up, just remember that there is a 10-year-old in San Francisco who felt the same way at times, but he chose *not* to give up and ultimately won the game.

If HE can do it, so can YOU!

ALL THE BEST!

5

ALL ABOUT RUBIK'S CUBE
NOTATIONS

F INALLY! We are about to learn how to solve the Rubik's Cube! Yay!

I hope you guys enjoy learning this amazing puzzle as much as I am enjoying trying to teach it to all of you.

And it does not matter even if you've never really held a Rubik's Cube in your hands. What I am about to tell you will make even the beginner Cube enthusiast understand how to get started.

Let us start with the basics first.

WHAT ARE EDGE PIECES, CENTER PIECES, AND CORNER PIECES?

A standard 3 x 3 Rubik's Cube consists of 26 small cubes, called pieces, and six faces. Each face has a piece at the center known as the centerpiece, so we have six centerpieces in all.

Edge pieces are the ones having pieces of two different colors. There are 12 edge pieces in all.

Finally, the pieces on each of the corners bear three differently colored pieces on their mutually orthogonal sides. In total, there are eight corner pieces.

Next, there are **two important facts** that I want you to know before we move further.

1. The centerpieces never move around about each other, although you can rotate them by rotating any face of the Cube. If you have a face with a red piece at the center, that will always be the red face. In other words, the piece in the center of the face determines the color of the cube face. When you're twisting and turning the Cube, you're not moving all the 54 pieces. You are only just moving 20 pieces—the 12 on the edges and the eight corner ones.

2. The second important fact every person trying to solve the Cube MUST know is that it is solved layer-by-layer and not face-by-face. Let me explain this with the help

of an example. Let us suppose you have an edge piece with a white piece and a blue piece, and you're using it to solve the white face. In this case, you have already started to solve the blue face too. So, whenever you are trying to solve a particular face, you are also simultaneously solving the first few pieces of four adjacent faces.

BASIC RUBIK'S CUBE MOVE NOTATIONS

As we all know, there are six sides to the Cube, and a certain angle can rotate each one. These rotations are called "moves" or sometimes "turns." You can rotate by 0, 90, 180, or -90 degrees.

The 90 degree and -90 degree moves are called "quarter turns," while the 180-degree move is called the "double turn." And if you rotate one side of the Cube, it is called "rotating a layer."

Now, to better understand or to write down the move sequences on the Cube, cubers use a notation of six main letters:

F for Front (the layer facing you)
B for Back (the layer facing away from you)
U for Up (the layer on the top)
D for Down (the layer at the bottom)
L for Left (the layer on your left)
R for Right (the layer on your right)

There are three other letters for notation as well that come in handy when learning to speed cube:

M for Middle (the layer between the left and right layers)

E for Equator (the layer between the top and bottom layers)

S for Standing (the layer between front and back layers)

Now, all of these letters are used in algorithms, or the sequences used to solve the Cube. A particular letter by itself tells you to rotate that layer clockwise by 90 degrees. For example, letter T says you need to rotate the top layer clockwise by 90 degrees.

When there is an apostrophe after the letter (like F' or U'), it asks you to move that face *counterclockwise* by 90 degrees.

Further, if a letter has the number 2 following it (F2 or U2), it means you are required to do a 180-degree rotation of that face (in any direction).

For a better understanding of these letters and moves, let us consider the following example:

If an algorithm says – F2 L B' D,' it means you need to rotate the front layer (F) by 180 degrees. You will rotate the left layer (L) by a quarter-turn (90 degrees) in the clockwise direction, followed by rotating the back layer (B), again by quarter-turn but in a counterclockwise direction, and finally rotating the down layer (D) by a quarter-turn in a clockwise direction.

Now re-read this again slowly.

See, I told you it is not going to be all that tough!

Fun Activity

F2 B2 U2 D2 L2 R2

Try out this algorithm on your unscrambled Rubik's Cube and impress your family and friends with the amazing checkerboard pattern that appears on each face!

And don't get startled if they already start gushing—what a smartie you are!

Point to Remember:

A very important point to remember while twisting and turning your Rubik's Cube is that you should perform each move as if you are looking directly at the face affected by the move.

Remember this always!

ADVANCED NOTATIONS

Now that you've understood the basic Rubik's Cube notations, let us move to the advanced ones. (Don't worry, they are just as simple!)

DOUBLE LAYER MOVES

We have those capital letter moves (F, B, U, D, L, R) and we also have their corresponding small letter moves.

Small letter moves are layer moves, which means a face goes along with its corresponding middle layer simultaneously.

Sometimes, a move uses a capital letter with "w" next to it in a small letter. For example, f and Fw mean the same thing.

Also, small letters can be followed by an apostrophe or a "2" (f' or f2), just like the regular turns. The meaning of the apostrophe and 2 remains the same as in the case of capital letter turns.

CUBE ROTATIONS

Cube rotations refer to the rotation of the entire Cube—they are not actual turns.

Just like in mathematics, the Cube can be rotated on X, Y, and Z axes. These notations include:

x – for rotating the Cube on the X-axis (Right and Left layers stay the same)

y – for rotating the Cube on the Y-axis (Up and Down layers stay the same)

z – for rotating the Cube on Z-axis (Front and Back layers stay the same)

So, friends, this is all about Rubik's Cube notations *and* rotations! Once you understand what these notations stand for, you will have no trouble decoding various Rubik's Cube algorithms.

Also, they are so much fun to try! So just take out your Cube and start practicing; I can guarantee that you will enjoy trying out these moves so much that you'll probably lose track of time. (I know I did!)

Please note that the advanced notations are unnecessary if all you wish to do is learn how to solve the Rubik's Cube. However, if you plan to learn to speedcube and hope to become a speedcuber one day, the advanced notations will help you tremendously.

6

HOW TO MAKE A FLOWER PATTERN WITH THE RUBIK'S CUBE

After getting familiar with the Rubik's Cube notations, are you ready for more?

In this chapter, I am about to teach you how to form an interesting pattern on the Rubik's Cube—the flower pattern.

The flower pattern is not just an easy pattern to form but will also teach you how to follow various algorithms to solve the Cube.

For those who have no idea what the flower pattern looks like, here is a picture that will help you out.

A flower pattern is one where, on any given face of the Cube, the centerpiece is one color, and the surrounding eight pieces are of another color.

Most people who pick up the Rubik's Cube and play with it for a while don't pick it up again. EVER.

We are not saying that this puzzle is not interesting enough or it is way too difficult for most people to understand the basics. It is just that people lack the commitment and the level of patience required to solve this mind-blowing puzzle.

Either that or they have yet to come across an easy-to-understand beginner's guide on how to solve the Rubik's Cube penned by a 10-year-old boy named Harrington Yeh! *winks*

Jokes apart, I strongly feel another reason why most young kids find it next to impossible to solve the Rubik's Cube is that most store-bought cubes come with an instruction pamphlet that is so confusing that kids tend to give up after a few tries.

My purpose in writing this book is to make the entire process of solving the Cube as simple and enjoyable for all of you as possible.

I do not want you to learn long, complicated algorithms. Instead, I want you to get through the entire process in an organic and super-interesting fashion.

QUICK RECAP

Before I get down to explaining how to form this pattern on your Cube, let us do a quick recap of the basics we learned in the previous chapter.

Each of the six faces of the Cube has three kinds of pieces: the centerpiece, four pieces on the corners, and four edge pieces (nine in all).

Now the edge pieces have two different colors, while the corner pieces have three colors on their mutually orthogonal sides.

COLOR SCHEME OF THE RUBIK'S CUBE

In the US, almost all Rubik's Cube models have the following colors opposite of each other:

- The orange face opposite the red face
- The green face opposite the blue face, and
- The white face opposite the yellow face

MAKING THE FLOWER PATTERN

Okay, now let's get down to making the flower pattern on a standard 3 x 3 Rubik's Cube.

I will not just be teaching you how to make this pattern but also how to bring back the Rubik's Cube to its unscrambled form.

Please note that I am teaching you how to make the flower pattern on your Rubik's Cube to get you introduced to the concept of algorithms and how they work. The flower pattern will prove to be super useful once we move onto the next chapters that explain the process of solving the Cube.

Just begin by taking the Rubik's Cube in your hands. It does not matter which color face is facing you.

Now all you have to do is perform the U notation, that is, move the upper layer clockwise by 90 degrees.

The next notation is D', which means you have to move the bottom layer counterclockwise by 90 degrees.

After this comes the next notation—R. This means you have to give the right layer a quarter-turn in the clockwise direction.

Next comes the L' notation that requires you to turn the left layer by 90 degrees counterclockwise.

The F notation follows this, so you need to give the front layer a quarter-turn clockwise.

After this comes B', which means you need to rotate the back face by 90 degrees counterclockwise.

Next comes the U notation that requires you to give a clockwise quarter-turn to the upper face.

The last notation that should reveal a beautiful pattern on your Rubik's Cube is D'. Move the bottom layer counterclockwise by 90 degrees.

Super simple, wasn't it? Just a few turns, and that's it!

So, the complete algorithm for making a flower pattern on a 3 x 3 Rubik's Cube is:

U D' R L' F B' U D'

You can never go wrong with this pattern if you follow this algorithm properly.

BRINGING BACK THE CUBE TO ITS SOLVED FORM

Now that your Rubik's Cube sits pretty with an attractive flower pattern displayed on each of its six faces, the question is how to bring it back to its solved form.

Well, that is pretty simple too.

To bring your Rubik's Cube back to its former position, you have to undo this scramble.

The first step in this direction would be to write the entire algorithm backward.

D' U B' F L' R D' U

The next step would be to apply the inverse rotations of this algorithm, which means that D' becomes D, and U becomes U'.

So, the algorithm for undoing this pattern would be:

D U' B F' L R' D U'

Super easy!

Fun Fact: *The flower pattern is referred to as the "Doughnut" by many cubers. What do you think about this? Which name suits the pattern more?*

So now that you know the algorithms of making the checkerboard pattern (we already discussed that in the last chapter) as well as the flower pattern on your Rubik's Cube, you can go ahead and impress your cousins and friends with your cool cubing skills.

Once you practice these patterns multiple times, your fingers will move automatically at surprising speed to form them. Also, when you start enjoying hanging out with your Cube, you might discover a few other ways of forming these patterns and several other interesting patterns too.

So, keep trying and having fun with your Rubik's Cube. I can assure you- once you get addicted to this little thing, there's no looking back!

7

MAKING THE WHITE CROSS

Okay, so now that you can make a flower pattern on your Rubik's Cube like a pro, let us take things a notch higher and march toward the first step in solving the Rubik's Cube.

Are you ready? Well, so am I!

As is true for most things in life, it is best to solve the Rubik's Cube by breaking the task into a series of smaller problems and then tackling each one by one.

We already discussed in Chapter 5 that it is best to solve the Rubik's Cube layer-by-layer, so the first step would be to start with the first layer and then gradually move to the middle and the bottom layer.

Now with the following two steps, you can solve the first layer:

- Creating the white cross
- Inserting the white corners

This chapter will teach you how to make the white cross on top of the Rubik's Cube. To get a clearer picture of what this means, look at the image below.

It is important to remember that when you make a white cross, the edge pieces on the other faces should correctly match their centerpieces, just as shown in the image below.

At this point, you can ignore the pieces that are grey in the image.

In case any of you are wondering why we are only talking about the *white* cross here, not the blue cross or the red cross—well, there *is* a reason for that.

It is always advisable to start solving the Cube with the white face at the top to always look out for the same colors at the next stages. For instance, when you start with the white face, you know that you have to look for yellow pieces to solve the last layer. Remembering the white face is opposite to the yellow face will greatly reduce the chances of getting confused.

Also, since most online tutorials and books also start with a white face at the top, this is an unspoken rule in Rubik's Cube Universe. But if you don't particularly like white color, or are much fonder of, say, the red color, you can start with that.

However, in this book, I am starting with the white face.

Okay, now let us get down to creating the white cross. Now that the truth is spoken, it is tough to explain exactly *how* to make the white cross since every person's cube is scrambled differently. I would recommend you spend some time trying to figure it out for yourself through trial and error. (It will be a great mental exercise, trust me!)

However, if after a few minutes your patience has started wearing thin, or if you're finding this too difficult, I am always here to help!

We have to first begin by holding the Cube with a white face on top (you should identify it from its white centerpiece).

Now, building a white cross is just a matter of inserting each of the four white edge pieces, one by one, around the white center.

I once again repeat, it is best if you manage to solve the cross on your own. It will not just be more interesting and fun, but you will learn quite a lot of exciting new things about the Cube.

However, if you are stuck, here is how to go about it.

The white edge pieces can be in any one of the following three positions:

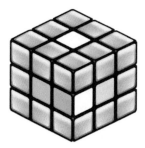

On the top layer

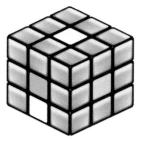

On the bottom layer

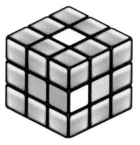

On the middle layer

In each of these cases, it does not matter which side of the edge piece is white, as we can always fix it later. What we will do is try to place each white edge piece on the white face, one after the other, without worrying too much about the order you're placing them.

First, you need to move the edge piece down to the bottom layer.

Next, align the piece directly under the white face where you want it to rotate the bottom layer.

If the white edge piece faces downwards or toward the side, use one of the below methods to move it to its correct position on the white face.

White piece facing down

If the edge piece is white and facing down, you simply have to line it directly under the place on the white face where you want it to go and then rotate the corresponding side face 180 degrees.

The white piece on the side

This one can be a bit tricky. In this case, we need to align the piece directly below where it should go and then rotate the bottom layer 90 degrees counterclockwise (D'). After that, rotate the front layer 90 degrees counterclockwise (F').

Next, give a quarter-turn to the right layer (R), and finally, rotate the front layer 90 degrees (F).

So, the algorithm for this becomes D' F' R F.

See how simple this was!

Suppose you were able to create the white cross without any help or guidance—GREAT! I am sure you must have felt awesome after you managed to do it all by yourself.

And if you needed a bit of guidance from this book, that is also completely okay. What matters is that you were persistent and patient enough to follow the directions and finally achieve your goal. So, congratulations to you too!

Now that we have taken the first step toward solving the Rubik's Cube by creating the white cross, it is time to move forward. But before that, let me remind you again—practice makes a person perfect, so practice, practice, practice.

Remember that the more time you spend with your Rubik's Cube, the better the chances of your being able to grasp the next steps quickly.

8

SOLVING THE BOTTOM CORNERS OF THE FIRST LAYER

By now, you know how to create the white cross on your Rubik's Cube. You also know that it wasn't remotely as difficult as it seemed, and you have started enjoying twisting and turning your Cube, with or without instructions.

In this chapter, we'll learn how to solve the first layer, meaning the white face.

You can solve this step intuitively by choosing to exercise your brain a little, or if you're feeling too lazy or if you're in a hurry to solve the Cube to impress your friend who keeps boasting about how smart he is, you can just follow the instructions below.

Coming back to the Cube, we already have the centerpiece and the edge pieces of the first layer in place; then, we need to bring the four corner pieces in the right place; this would solve our first layer.

As you already know by now, corner pieces have three edges. So, for completing the white face, you need the corner pieces that have one white piece.

Before we move further, let me tell you that there are two ways of doing this step. Some people prefer to do it with the white cross facing upwards, while some prefer to solve it with the white cross facing down. Both the ways are correct; it all boils down to personal preference.

However, I will teach you how to solve the first layer with the white cross facing down for this book's purposes. The reason behind this is that it would be much easier for you to understand what is going on, as you will easily see all three colored pieces on the corner pieces that are to be placed in their right position for solving the white face.

Now, the white panel (or piece) on these corner pieces can be in any one of the following three orientations:

White piece on top

White piece facing toward the front

White piece facing toward the side

To slot each corner piece in its right place, you have to make sure the white part of it is always on your front right (and, of course, the white cross is at the bottom) as shown in the image below:

However, if the piece is not oriented correctly, you need to perform the following algorithm to ensure it faces you.

U R U' U' R'

Keep performing this algorithm repeatedly until the white piece starts facing you.

Once that is done, perform the following algorithm, and your white corner will be solved.

U R U' R'

Alternatively, you can solve the first layer using another method.

In this method, if you have the white piece to your front right, you need to perform the following algorithm to slot it into its right position.

R' F R F'

And just in case the white piece is not on your right front and is facing upwards, that's okay too. Just keep repeating the algorithm mentioned above until it comes to the right place.

By slotting each corner piece one-by-one into their places, you will solve your white face, or the first layer. Super easy!

Please note that at the end of this step, your Rubik's Cube should look like the image below:

If it does, congratulations—you can now move on to the next stage in style!

But before we move further, let us talk about the algorithms that we just used to solve the first layer. An interesting thing that you might have noticed in the algorithms listed above is they're very simple to memorize since there is asymmetry; this makes solving the Cube much easier and more fun.

Now that you've learned how to use the algorithms to solve the first layer, you should still try the trial-and-error method. The trial-and-error method is not only more interesting, but it will also enhance your problem-solving skills and make your brain sharper as a result.

What's more, the satisfaction that you will derive from knowing you managed to do it all on your own would be unparalleled!

9

SOLVING SECOND LAYER EDGES

W e have managed to complete the first layer, or the white face, and we are moving toward the next layer.

Before solving the second layer, the centerpieces should already be in place, so we have to place the second layer edge pieces in their right position. Sounds simple, doesn't it? And it is, trust me!

SECOND LAYER PIECES

Okay, now let us get started. Just like we did in the last chapter, here too, we will turn the Rubik's Cube upside down (white face facing down). Turning the Rubik's cube upside down is important as it will help you see the colored pieces on the remaining pieces easily and make you better understand what you are doing.

Now, as you hold the upside-down Cube in your hands, it is the yellow face that will be up. And how will you know it is the yellow face?

That's right—from the yellow centerpiece. (You are getting smarter already!)

Okay, now looking at the top layer, find out the second layer pieces that need to move to their right location.

For explanation purposes, we will take the example of blue and red edge pieces.

Blue Inverted T

When you locate the blue-red edge piece on the top layer, rotate the top layer until it forms an upside-down "T". Depending upon which way the piece is oriented, the inverted T can be in any of the following two ways:

Red Inverted T

This edge piece (on the top layer) needs to go in its right place, between the red and blue faces.

In the first picture above (blue T) the piece would need to move to the right edge, and in the second picture (red T) the piece would go to the left edge.

We have different algorithms for both of these situations.

If you want to move the edge piece on the top layer to the right, the algorithm would be:

U R U' R' U' F' U F

On the other hand, if the top layer edge piece needs to be moved left, the algorithm would be:

U' L' U L U F U' F'

Using these algorithms, you should be able to solve the second-layer edge pieces.

But wait, there is more!

SPECIAL CASES

There can be times when the second layer tries to play smart with you and presents you with a tricky situation, like this:

In this scenario, no second layer edge piece seems to be in the right place (or even if it is in the right place, the orientation may be wrong), so making an inverted T looks kind of impossible.

But don't you worry, we have a solution for that too!

To fix this seemingly *complex* situation, just perform any of the two above-listed algorithms.

If you use the first algorithm, the yellow-red edge piece will move right and will displace the orange-green piece, which will, in turn, move to the top layer.

Now that the orange-green piece is in the top layer, you can rotate the top layer and solve it normally by forming a green inverted T.

Wait, this isn't over yet!

There is another situation that you might encounter while solving the second layer. It's what happens when your Cube looks like *this*:

Can you think of how to solve this situation? Think, think, think.

Did you manage to solve it?

If not, let me help you out.

You once again need to use the first algorithm mentioned above to displace the red-blue piece. Once that piece moves to the top layer, you can solve this using the method mentioned above.

So, with this we just learned how to solve the second layer too! I am sure that you must have tons of fun trying out different algorithms on the Cube by now. The task looks daunting initially, but as you pay attention and move step by step, it becomes super interesting and even kind of addictive.

Okay, let me ask you guys something. Did you understand why we started solving the second layer with the Cube turned upside down? Didn't it make solving the second layer edges much more convenient?

If you feel confident enough, try solving this layer with the white face up. It is going to be more challenging, but fun nevertheless.

Remember that unless we do something that challenges our minds, we are unlikely to unlock its true potential.

10

SOLVING THE LAST LAYER EDGES

Y ou must be super excited, right? After all, you are just a few minutes away from solving the Rubik's Cube for the first time!

Now since you are almost there, let us talk about what you need to do first to solve the third and final layer of the Rubik's Cube.

To solve the last layer, meaning the yellow layer of the Cube, take these two steps:

1. Solving the last layer edges
2. Solving the last layer corners

We will take up the second step in the next chapter.

FORMING A YELLOW CROSS

And no, before you start feeling too happy that this is similar to how you solved the white cross, let me tell you this is different. Very different. So different that if you start doing it the white-cross way, there are bright chances that you will end up messing up your Rubik's Cube to the point of no return, which essentially means that all the hard work you've done goes down the drain.

Are you shuddering at the thought of it? Well, who wouldn't?

Okay, so taking things further (in the right direction)—to form a yellow cross on the last layer, you need to first identify which of the following four conditions apply to your Cube:

Can you spot a Backward L, like this?

Or is there a line like this?

Or a dot, like this?

Or a yellow cross, like this?

Let us talk about each of the above-listed four conditions one by one.

BACKWARD L

If you can spot a Backward L on the last layer, you need to perform the below-listed algorithm. However, make sure that you are holding your Cube so that the L shape is in the top left.

F U R U' R' F'

LINE

If there is a line on the yellow face, you have to hold the Cube in such a manner that the line looks horizontal and then perform the following algorithm:

F R U R' U' F'

DOT

If there is a dot-like pattern on the last layer (as shown in the pictures above), you have to use both these algorithms in whichever order you please.

If you choose to apply the Backward L algorithm first, you'll get a line that you can then solve using the line algorithm.

Alternatively, if you choose to use the line algorithm first, it will produce a Backward L shape on the last layer, so you can solve using the first algorithm.

A point to remember here is that no matter which algorithm you choose to apply first, just make sure you are holding your Rubik's Cube in the right way. The Backward L shape should be on the top left corner, and the line should be horizontal.

YELLOW CROSS

For those of you who are lucky enough, you might already have a yellow cross on your last layer! If that is the case, you need not worry about any algorithms and straightaway move ahead to solve the last layer edges.

ALIGNING THE LAST LAYER EDGES

In this step, we will need to move the edges of the yellow cross that we just created so that the edge pieces align with the centerpieces. Just like this:

To move ahead, you need to first determine which of the edge pieces need to be moved. You can do this by rotating the yellow face until you get two edge pieces that align correctly with their center pieces. For instance, in the picture shown above, the red and blue edge pieces are right next to the center pieces of the same color.

Now, what about the remaining two edge pieces?

Well, if you have a Rubik's Cube in hand where the remaining two edge pieces also align perfectly with their center pieces, congratulations! You can move to the next chapter right away!

If not, then these remaining two edge pieces will have to be moved to their right places so that they are also positioned next to the center pieces of the same color.

Now there can be two possibilities here:

1. The two edge pieces that are incorrectly placed are adjacent to each other, like this:

In this case, you need to first rotate the Cube in such a manner that the incorrectly placed edged pieces are on the Front and Right faces. Once you do that, apply the following algorithm:

U R U R' U R U2 R'

2. The two edge pieces that are incorrectly placed are opposite to each other, like this:

In this case, you just need to apply the same algorithm, but twice. When you perform it the first time, you will see that the incorrect edge pieces come adjacent to each other. So, performing the algorithm again will bring them to their positions.

Again, remember to rotate the Cube before applying the algorithm the second time so that the incorrectly placed edged pieces are on the Front and Right faces.

After doing all of this, you will be holding a Rubik's Cube with two layers solved, and the third layer with a yellow cross and all the edge pieces in the right places.

You are now soooo close to solving the Rubik's Cube! All you need to do is move the last layer corners to the right places and voila! You will be among the 5.8% of the world population that has actually managed to solve the Rubik's Cube!

If that is not something to be immensely proud of, I don't know what is!

SPECIAL CASES

Some people might struggle with making the yellow cross because their Cube might end up looking like any of these:

If that person is you, I am sorry to say that your Cube cannot be solved.

And no, I am not joking.

The reason behind any of the above "special case" situations could be that your Cube has been previously disassembled and reassembled randomly. (I know quite a few people who've done that, *just for fun*!)

When that happens, the chances of the Cube becoming unsolvable become 91.6%.

So, if you find yourself stuck with a Cube that looks unsolvable, you have two options to set things right:

You can disassemble your Cube (many YouTube videos will help you out) and then reassemble it in the solved position. Once reassembled, you can scramble it again and then try to solve it right from the beginning.

I know this might sound tough, especially when you're already holding a mostly solved Cube in your hands, but don't give in! Believe me, you're almost at the end of this, so you don't want to quit now.

The second solution would be to peel off the pieces and put them back in the right place.

Let me remind you that you will find yourself in such a position *only* if your Rubik's Cube has been ruined by disassembling and random reassembling.

11

SOLVING THE LAST LAYER CORNERS

O kay, so we are *finally* here!

We are now at the last and final stage of solving the Rubik's Cube, and this involves moving all four corners to their correct places.

STEP 1

The first step in this stage involves just moving the corners to their right place, even if the orientation is incorrect. So, your Cube should be looking something like this:

At this point, what you first need to check is whether any of the corner pieces in the third layer are already in their right position. For example, in the picture above, you can notice that the red-blue-yellow corner piece is in its right place (between red, blue, and yellow faces) even though it is not facing the correct way.

Now let me tell you an important fact. At this stage, **if there are any correct corners, you will have either one or all four of them.**

If all the four corners are in the correct place, you can congratulate yourself and move on to the next step.

If there is just one correct corner, you should hold the Cube so that it is positioned in the FRU corner. Before you scratch your head and ask where this FRU corner is, it is the corner formed by the Front, Right, and Up faces.

In the picture above, the red-blue-yellow corner piece is in the FRU corner.

If you have no corner pieces in the right place, then it doesn't matter which corner piece lies in the FRU corner.

In the third case scenario (no pieces in the correct place), you need to perform the following algorithm:

U R U' L' U R' U' L

When you apply this algorithm, the three corner pieces (except the one in the FRU corner) will change places so that you will have at least one in the correct place.

Once that happens, hold the Cube so that the correct piece is in the FRU corner, and repeat the algorithm.

If you already started with one correct corner piece in the FRU corner (second case scenario) and the other corners still not in their right places, you should apply the algorithm again.

By applying the algorithm, you will ensure that all the corners are now in their right places.

What we need to do now is to ensure that all the corners have their yellow piece facing up to complete the yellow face. Once that is done, the Cube will be solved!

STEP 2

If you remember, in the first step you had to find a correct corner piece and then make sure it is in the FRU corner.

In this step, you have to locate an *incorrect* corner piece first. Here, "incorrect" means a corner piece that does not have the yellow piece facing up (since our ultimate goal is to have *all* the corner pieces with their yellow pieces facing up).

Once you locate an incorrect corner piece, hold the Cube in such a manner that it moves to the FRU corner, like this:

In the above picture, you can see three incorrect corner pieces (ones that do not have the yellow side up), and one of them is in the FRU corner.

Now, where the yellow side of the incorrect corner piece is facing is extremely important.

There can only be two possibilities: the yellow side is either facing right or it's facing forward.

Of course, the yellow side can also face up, but if that is the case, it wouldn't be considered an incorrect corner piece in the first place!

So, let us talk about the other two possibilities:

- If the yellow side is facing to the right (as shown in the image below), you need to apply the following algorithm:

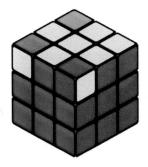

R' D' R D R' D' R D

On noticing carefully, you will find that this algorithm is basically R' D' R D repeated twice.

- If the yellow side is facing toward the front (as shown

in the image below), you will need to apply the following algorithm:

R' D' R D R' D' R D R' D' R D R' D' R D

Don't be alarmed by this algorithm's length—it is just the previous algorithm repeated twice (or just R' D' R D four times)!

I know that when you apply these algorithms, you will see the bottom two layers getting messed up.

Don't panic. (It is hard not to panic after you've reached this point but trust me!) These layers know how to sort themselves out as you go further.

Once a particular incorrect corner piece is solved (that is, it gets correctly oriented), you can move to the next incorrect corner piece.

But before doing that, remember this extremely important point:

Do not rotate the whole Cube to move the next incorrect piece to the FRU corner.

I repeat, it is extremely important that you understand this.

Instead of rotating the whole Cube, you only need to use U, or U', or U2 to ensure the next incorrect corner piece moves to the FRU corner.

Once the next incorrect piece is in the FRU corner, you need to perform the above-listed algorithms, again depending on where the yellow side is facing.

When all your corner pieces have their yellow sides up, just rotate the upper layer (as required) to complete all the Cube faces.

CONGRATULATIONS!

YOU JUST SOLVED YOUR RUBIK'S CUBE FOR THE VERY FIRST TIME!

WHAT NEXT?

Okay, so you can now consider yourself as one of the few people on this planet (5.8% really is just a few) who can claim to have solved the Rubik's Cube!

Solving the cube is a commendable achievement indeed, but one should not rest on their laurels, as they say.

So, the next step would be to keep practicing.

I know it might take some time before you can unscramble the Cube without referring to the algorithms, but with persistent practice and patience, you can do it.

Most cubers (including me!) say that they took several minutes to solve their Cube initially, but with continuous practice, they could bring their solve times down to a few seconds.

If you dream of becoming a speedcuber someday, the next chapter will guide you in the right direction.

12

SOME TIPS ON HOW TO SOLVE THE RUBIK'S CUBE MORE QUICKLY

E ver since the Rubik's Cube's first introduction to the world, it intrigued the minds of thousands of people. But there is one question that every person who learns how to solve it asks. "What next?"

Are you asking that question too?

I know how to solve the Cube now; what should I do next?

Well, how about trying to solve it *more quickly?*

Before moving further, just answer these questions. Can you manage to solve the Cube unaided now? Can you consistently manage to solve it in less than two minutes? Are you hooked on this puzzle so much that you keep toying with it in your free time? Are you eager to learn more about the Cube?

If your answer to all of these questions is yes, then it is time to move ahead. You should now aim to improve your solve time and try to impress your friends and family further by solving the Cube in a matter of seconds.

I am enlisting a few tips and tricks below that will help you to improve your solving time of the Rubik's Cube significantly. These tips are specifically for beginners who use the method explained in this book to solve the Cube, although the tips can prove beneficial for more experienced solvers.

Now, I am not saying that learning these tricks will help you break any speedcubing records, but they will help you improve your solving times and bring them down to anywhere from 20 to 60 seconds.

That's pretty impressive for a kid who has only just learned how to solve the Rubik's Cube!

So, without any further ado, let us get started. Here are some important tips that will help you lower your solving time of the Cube.

PRACTICE. PRACTICE. PRACTICE

As I have said multiple times before, practice is the only way to become a Rubik's Cube expert. Without sufficient practice, you will just not be able to bring down your solving time. So, keep practicing whenever you have free time.

In my case, I did not need anyone to motivate me to practice. I was so obsessed with the Cube that I carried it with me at all times. I used to keep twisting and turning my Cube, so I learned much through hit-and-trial.

But I understand that not everyone will be that crazy about this puzzle. I am listing more tips below that will make your practice much more effective.

But again, you have to keep in mind that these tips will be of help *only* if you practice them enough.

MAKE USE OF FINGER TRICKS

I know, you probably haven't heard the term "finger tricks" before, so here is what it means.

Finger tricks mean performing a particular move or rotation using just one finger instead of the whole hand. So, if you have to perform the U or U' notations (which, by the way, are the easiest notations when it comes to finger tricks), you just use your right/left index finger and not your entire hand.

The main goal of using finger tricks is to lower your execution time. It is obvious that if you execute notations using fingers only, the execution time will fall.

And with continuous practice, most finger tricks will come naturally to you. Yes, some will not come as easily and will be a little tougher to execute but, with practice, you can master those too and bring down your algorithm execution time.

MAKE SURE YOUR RUBIK'S CUBE IS OF HIGH QUALITY

As basic as this may sound, it is an important factor to consider if you seriously want to learn how to cube faster.

Two factors determine your solve time: you and your Rubik's Cube. Let's talk about the latter here.

A Rubik's Cube that is not well made will be difficult to twist and turn, significantly lowering your solving time. The chances of it getting stuck while you're solving are also high.

It is extremely important that your Rubik's Cube is of high quality; it should move as smooth as butter. This will make practice much more fun and make implementing finger tricks super easy.

USE LUBE

No matter how buttery smooth your Rubik's Cube is, it starts losing its smoothness after hours of practice. I cannot say for sure, but I believe the reason behind that is dust/dirt, or maybe just regular wear and tear.

You may find your good quality Cube also getting locked up if your fingers are moving too fast on it.

So, what can be the solution to this problem?

Well, it turns out that there *is* a way to help your Cube retain its smoothness. You can use special Rubik's Cube lubes that ensure the mechanism inside the puzzle moves without any friction. Speedcubers use this all the time to make sure their Cube moves as fast as their hands.

LEARN ALGORITHMS BY HEART

Remembering the algorithm is basic, and this is something you can achieve only through practice.

To solve the Cube faster, you *have to* memorize the algorithms and then execute them multiple times. You will find out that after you practice a particular algorithm a few times, you will be able to execute it without even thinking about the notations, just using your "hands memory."

Think of it as typing on a keyboard. Once you become familiar with typing through consistent practice, your fingers move of their own accord, without your even giving a thought about each letter's location on the keyboard.

TRY TO MINIMIZE CUBE ROTATIONS

Just to remind you, cube rotation means turning the entire Cube clockwise or counterclockwise around its vertical axis.

When we execute a cube rotation, it costs valuable time while doing nothing to bring the Cube closer to its unscrambled state. Most speedcubers aim to minimize their cube rotations to save this precious time.

I know attempting to minimize cube rotations will take some practice, especially since you have become used to rotating the Cube to gain positional leverage. But once you are determined to try to solve the Cube without rotating it, you'll find out that it is not as tough as it seems.

When I was learning to speedcube, I tried the same approach and found that with consistent practice, I could (more comfortably) solve pieces on the back face of the cube rather than rotating it 180 degrees to solve them in the front.

LOOK INTO THE FUTURE

No, I am not talking about gaining some mystical powers here. All I mean is you should try to think ahead when it comes to solving the Rubik's Cube.

Allow me to explain this in detail.

If you think carefully, solving time is made up of two things: the time involved in applying a particular algorithm and the time you spend *before* applying the algorithm, which involves searching for the next piece to be solved, which algorithm to apply next, etc.

Now, the time involved in applying any algorithm can only be brought down with continuous practice, as I keep repeating. The more you practice, the better your solving time will become.

But when it comes to the time you spend *thinking* before applying the algorithm, well, you may not be aware of this, but this effort forms a significant part of the total solving time.

So, what to do to reduce this "thinking" time? An important and useful tip for bringing down your thinking time would be to start looking for the next pieces to be solved while executing an algorithm.

This is essential. While performing any algorithm, instead of just focusing on the pieces you are solving, look a little ahead and start searching for pieces you're going to solve next. To do this, you would need to slow down your speed a bit as you move toward the end of an algorithm, so that it becomes easier to locate the next piece to be solved while your fingers are still working on the current algorithm.

You must be thinking that these are tips to lower your solving time but here I am, talking about slowing down your speed toward the end of each algorithm. Trust me, this slowing down will triple its value because of the time it reduces in the thinking part. Even the best speedcubers use this method to lower their solve times.

For example, let us assume you are solving the middle layer edges. In this step, instead of completely focusing on solving the edge piece, start looking for the edge piece that needs to be solved next. With practice, you'll be able to locate it even before you've completed the current algorithm.

Planning saves precious time and allows you to immediately start working on the next algorithm without any time lag.

Again, I know this will not come easily or quickly to you as it requires quite a bit of practice. But once you start understanding how to do this, there will be no looking back. I can guarantee that your solve time will drastically fall once you get the hang of this planning trick.

TRY TO BE COLOR NEUTRAL

Are you scratching your head again? Well, color neutrality is all about starting to solve with any color instead of a particular color.

For example, most people start solving the Rubik's Cube with the white face first (as explained in this book, too). When I was new to cubing, I always started forming a cross on the white side first.

While this method is great for beginners who are just learning how to solve the Rubik's Cube, it may not be the most efficient one (especially when it comes to speedcubing).

When a cuber is color neutral, they do not necessarily begin solving the Cube with the white face. Since each scramble is unique, cubers should carefully assess which side is the easiest to solve and then begin with that face. By easiest to solve, I mean choosing a side that helps solve the Cube faster, with fewer moves.

That easiest face could be white, but it could also be one of the remaining five colors.

In short, to become a color-neutral cuber, you should be able to determine which color is the easiest to start with for a particular scramble (something that you can only achieve after consistent practice). And then, you should be able to achieve the same level of competency in solving the Cube no matter which color you start with.

If you are wondering why I am telling you this after explaining how to solve the Rubik's Cube by forming the white cross first, it's because my initial aim was to teach you the basics of Cube solving.

Now I'm assuming that you are competent enough to solve the Cube unaided after tons of practice and want to move ahead and try speedcubing as well. When it comes to speedcubing, the earlier you start practicing color neutrality, the easier it will be for you.

The more comfortable you get solving the Cube starting with one particular color, the harder it becomes to unlearn that and start with another color.

I highly recommend trying to solve the Cube starting with different colors each time. It is quite easy, and it will help you immensely if you seriously care about bringing down your solving times.

THE MOST COMMON SPEEDCUBING METHOD: CFOP

The most common speedcubing method is called CFOP, or the Fridrich's Method.

As the name suggests, Jessica Fridrich (remember her?) developed this method. She is the one who uploaded her method of solving the Cube on the Internet in 1997 and whose page became wildly popular among Cube enthusiasts in the early 2000s.

The name CFOP comes from the four steps involved in this method:

1. Cross
2. F2L (First Two Layers)
3. OLL (Orient the Last Layer)
4. PLL (Permute the Last Layer)

This method can get you down to around 25 seconds or even faster. As you can see, it is very similar to the method that I have already explained in detail in this book. However, each step is a bit different.

Assuming that you are still a beginner for Cube solving, I suggest you stick to the beginner's method (the one this book explains in detail).

You can use the tips and tricks listed above to improve your solving times, and of course, you should practice as much as you can. You should try the CFOP method after mastering the beginner's method.

13

A QUICK RECAP OF ALL THE ALGORITHMS

I n this chapter, let us quickly go through ALL the algorithms listed in this book.

This chapter will be a quick reference guide if you only wish to look up the algorithms that need to be applied at every step.

THE TWO PATTERNS

So, let us begin with the **algorithms for the two patterns** first:

Checkerboard Pattern

F2 B2 U2 D2 L2 R2

R2 L2 D2 U2 B2 F2 (TO UNDO)

Flower Pattern

U D' R L' F B' U D'

D U' B F' L R' D U' (TO UNDO)

LAYER BY LAYER

Now let us quickly recap all the **algorithms involved in solving the Rubik's Cube**:

Making the White Cross

In case the edge piece has a white piece facing sidewards, you need to align it directly below where it is meant to go, and then apply this algorithm:

D' F' R F

First Layer Corners

To reorient the corner pieces correctly for the bottom layer (white, as we are holding the Cube in such a manner that the white cross faces down), apply this algorithm:

U R U' U' R'

To insert the corner pieces in their right place on the bottom layer, apply this algorithm:

U R U' R'

Second Layer Edges

In the case of the second layer, the center pieces are already in place so all we have to do is place the second layer edge pieces in their right position.

For moving an edge piece on the top layer to the right, apply this algorithm:

U R U' R' U' F' U F

For moving an edge piece on the top layer to the left, apply this algorithm:

U' L' U L U F U' F'

Last Layer Edges

If you spot a **Backward L** on the last layer, apply this algorithm (make sure that you are holding your Cube in such a manner that the L shape is in the top left):

F U R U' R' F'

If there is a **line** on the yellow face, hold the Cube in such a manner that the line looks horizontal, and then apply this algorithm:

F R U R' U' F'

If there is a **yellow dot** on the last layer, you have to use both these algorithms, in whichever order you please.

F U R U' R' F'
F R U R' U' F'

If you choose to apply the Backward L algorithm first, you'll get a line that you can then solve using the line algorithm.

Alternatively, if you choose to use the line algorithm first, it will produce a Backward L shape on the last layer, which you can solve using the first algorithm.

Now, to switch incorrectly placed edge pieces on the top layer that are **adjacent to each other**, apply this algorithm:

U R U R' U R U2 R' (make sure the incorrectly placed edged pieces are on the Front and Right faces)

To switch incorrectly placed edge pieces on the top layer that are **opposite to each other**, apply this algorithm:

U R U R' U R U2 R' U R U R' U R U2 R' (the same algorithm, twice)

Last Layer Corners

When no corner pieces are in the correct place, apply this algorithm:

U R U' L' U R' U' L

When the yellow side of a corner piece is facing right instead of up, apply this algorithm:

R' D' R D R' D' R D (this is just R' D' R D twice)

When the yellow side is facing left, apply this algorithm:

R' D' R D R' D' R D R' D' R D R' D' R D (this is just R' D' R D four times)

So, these are all the algorithms you need to practice for solving the Rubik's Cube.

And with this, we move toward the end of this book...

CONCLUSION

As this book heads toward its end, I once again want to congratulate you on learning how to solve the Rubik's Cube. Solving the cube is a feat that few people have achieved, so **you should be proud of yourself!**

I sincerely hope that all of you had as much fun learning the entire process of solving the Cube as I had explaining it to you. I tried to simplify each step as much as possible so that even those of you who had never held a Rubik's Cube in their hands before could easily follow the instructions.

My main aim in writing this book was to make you aware of how exciting and fun this puzzle is, and how it can make you smarter by improving your muscle memory.

Now that you have seen for yourself how amazing the best-selling toy in history is, I highly recommend you keep twisting and turning it until you discover your own unique ways of solving it.

If you enjoyed reading this book, or if it simplified the process of learning how to solve the Rubik's Cube for you, don't forget to leave your review on Amazon!

I would absolutely LOVE to hear back from you.

I wish you the best always!

Harrington Yeh

Made in the USA
Middletown, DE
24 October 2021

50926462R00077